D1736648

th America

COYOTES

by Tammy Gagne

FOCUS
READERS

www.northstareditions.com

Produced for North Star Editions by Red Line Editorial.

Photographs ©: Images by Dr. Alan Lipkin/Shutterstock Images, cover, 1; Debbie Steinhausser/Shutterstock Images, 4–5; Len Jellicoe/iStockphoto, 8–9; Terje Langeland/Shutterstock Images, 11; KiraGunderson/iStockphoto, 12, 29; Josef Pittner/Shutterstock Images, 14–15, 27 (bottom left); NaturesMomentsuk/Shutterstock Images, 17; TheGreenMan/Shutterstock Images, 18; Tom Reichner/Shutterstock Images, 20–21; Jeannette Katzir Photog/Shutterstock Images, 22–23; critterbiz/Shutterstock Images, 25; mlharing/iStockphoto, 27 (top); Kane513/Shutterstock Images, 27 (bottom right)

ISBN
978-1-63517-034-4 (hardcover)
978-1-63517-090-0 (paperback)
978-1-63517-193-8 (ebook pdf)
978-1-63517-143-3 (hosted ebook)

Library of Congress Control Number: 2016951005

Printed in the United States of America
Mankato, MN
November, 2016

About the Author

Tammy Gagne has written more than 150 books for adults and children. She resides in northern New England with her husband and son. One of her favorite pastimes is visiting schools to talk to kids about the writing process.

TABLE OF CONTENTS

CHAPTER 1

AT HOME ANYWHERE

At one time, coyotes lived only in the central United States and most of Mexico. Today this **species** is found nearly all across North America. Coyotes live in deserts and prairies.

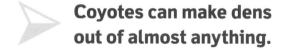

Coyotes can make dens out of almost anything.

Pacific
Ocean

North
America

Atlantic
Ocean

□ where coyotes live

N
W E
S

Coyotes live across almost all of North America.

They also wander in forests and

mountain areas.

Coyotes can live almost

anywhere. Some make dens in

caves. Others take over the dens

of other animals. Coyotes in **urban** areas even make homes out of storm drains.

Coyotes rarely stay in one place for long. Parents often move their pups from one den to another. This helps protect the pups from being discovered by **predators**.

FUN FACT

Some coyotes dig underground dens. These hidden resting places can be up to 30 feet (9.1 m) long.

CHAPTER 2

BLENDING IN

Most coyotes stand 15 to 20 inches (38 to 51 cm) tall. Adults are 32 to 37 inches (81 to 94 cm) from head to **rump**. They weigh 20 to 50 pounds (9 to 23 kg).

 A coyote is about as big as a medium-sized dog.

A coyote has large ears shaped like triangles. Each coyote also has a long, narrow **muzzle** with a black nose. Its thick coat is grayish-brown. Its belly has more white fur than the rest of its body.

A coyote's coloring depends on its environment. Coyotes living in the desert have lighter coats than coyotes in the mountains. The different coat colors help them blend in with their surroundings.

This coyote blends into the desert's sand and plants.

PARTS OF A COYOTE

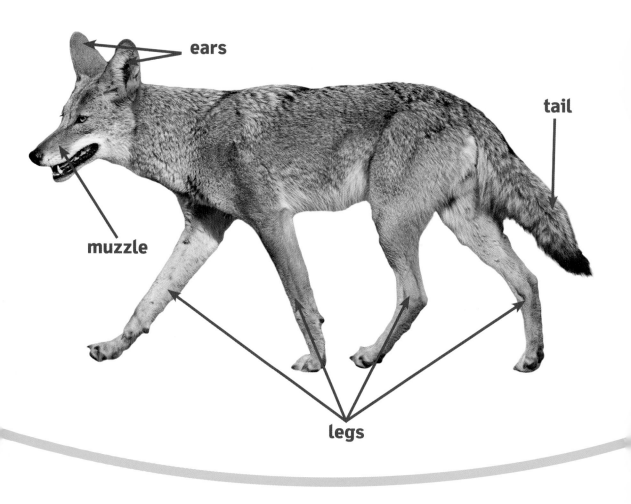

ears

tail

muzzle

legs

A coyote's bushy tail is approximately 16 inches (41 cm) long. Most coyotes have black tips

Coyotes are nicknamed prairie wolves. This is because they look similar to small, thin wolves.

at the end of their tails. Another black spot is usually found at the base of the spine. Coyotes have thin legs and small feet.

CHAPTER 3

BUILT TO SURVIVE

Coyotes live in a wide variety of **habitats** and climates. The animal's fur, muscles, and claws all help it survive in different areas. A coyote's thick coat keeps it warm during the winter.

 Thick hair keeps coyotes warm in the snow.

Coyotes can survive
in temperatures as cold as
−30 degrees Fahrenheit (−34°C).

In late spring, the animal sheds much of its hair. A thinner coat helps the coyote stay cool in the summer.

Coyotes are strong swimmers and fast runners. When hunting, coyotes can run up to 30 miles per hour (48 km/h).

A coyote runs through the snow.

Coyotes sometimes stick their muzzles underground to get prey.

Coyotes pant like dogs to cool down.

Their sharp eyesight, hearing, and sense of smell help lead coyotes to nearby **prey**. They can even locate a mouse hiding far underneath the snow. Once they catch their prey, coyotes use their claws to tear into it.

COYWOLVES

During the last century, it seemed that the coyotes in the eastern United States and Canada were getting bigger. The eastern coyotes had longer legs, larger jaws, and smaller ears than those in the western part of North America. Some people described them as more wolflike.

Scientists learned that these animals are part wolf. Coyotes in the east have mated with wolves for approximately the last 100 years. They are called coywolves. More than one million coywolves now live in this part of North America.

Coywolves are also called eastern coyotes.

CHAPTER 4

PART OF THE PACK

Coyotes eat a wide variety of foods. Their diet usually includes rabbits, dead animals, and rodents such as rats. They also eat fruits such as apples, grapes, and berries.

Coyotes howl to communicate with members of their pack.

A hungry coyote will eat whatever it can find or kill. In a pinch, even insects will do.

Coyotes live in packs of three or more. Coyotes usually hunt in pairs. The two partners may wander up to 200 feet (61 m) apart. Once they locate prey, they both move

FUN FACT

A coyote often buries a meal if it cannot eat it all. It comes back and digs it up when it is ready to finish eating.

 A coyote prepares to bite down on a pheasant.

closer to it. Several pairs of coyotes
may work together to hunt larger
animals such as deer.

Mother coyotes usually give birth to five to seven pups. Male and female coyotes raise their pups together in the spring. They make a den. When the pups are approximately nine weeks old, both parents teach them how to hunt.

The family stays together until fall. Then the young coyotes venture out into the world. They form new packs. A coyote can live up to 15 years.

COYOTE LIFE CYCLE

A mother gives birth to pups in spring. They stay in or near the den.

After a year, the young coyotes find new packs.

The mother and father teach their pups to hunt.

FOCUS ON
COYOTES

Write your answers on a separate piece of paper.

1. Summarize Chapter 2 of this book.

2. Do you think coywolves is a good name for coyotes that have mated with wolves? Why or why not?

3. Mother coyotes usually have how many pups at one time?
   A. one to three
   B. three to five
   C. five to seven

4. Why do coyotes have a varied diet?
   A. because it gives them more food options
   B. because they get sick of eating the same food
   C. because they want to steal food from other animals

5. What does **sheds** mean in this book?

    A. grows

    B. cuts

    C. loses

In late spring, the animal **sheds** much of its hair. A thinner coat helps the coyote stay cool in the summer.

6. What does **environment** mean in this book?

    A. moods

    B. surroundings

    C. age

A coyote's coloring depends on its **environment**. Coyotes living in the desert have lighter coats than coyotes in the mountains.

Answer key on page 32.

GLOSSARY

habitats
The type of places where plants or animals normally grow or live.

muzzle
An animal's nose and mouth.

predators
Animals that kill and eat other animals.

prey
An animal that is hunted and eaten by a different animal.

rump
The back part of an animal's body.

species
A group of animals or plants that are similar.

urban
Relating to a city environment.

TO LEARN MORE

BOOKS

Avett, Harper. *Coyotes*. New York: PowerKids Press, 2016.

Editors of Animal Planet. *Animal Planet Animal Atlas*. New York: Liberty Street, 2016.

Niver, Heather Moore. *Coyotes after Dark*. New York: Enslow Publishing, 2016.

NOTE TO EDUCATORS

Visit **www.focusreaders.com** to find lesson plans, activities, links, and other resources related to this title.

INDEX

Answer Key: 1. Answers will vary; **2.** Answers will vary; **3.** C; **4.** A; **5.** C; **6.** B